THE
Welcome Table

by Katherine S. Miller

This book is presented to

_____

by

_____

_____

(date)

AUGSBURG FORTRESS, MINNEAPOLIS

THE WELCOME TABLE:
Holy Communion Instruction for Children

Child's Book

Developed in cooperation with the Division for Congregational Ministries of the Evangelical Lutheran Church in America.

Writer: Katherine S. Miller
Editors: Beverly Riis Sperry and Virginia Bonde Zarth
Illustrator/designer: Len Ebert

SPECIAL DAYS, SPECIAL MEALS

When my brother and I got baptized, the pastor marked us with a cross. It was made with oil on our foreheads. Pastor made my cross first, and then my baby brother Joel's.

I checked his forehead. I could see where the shiny oil looked like a cross. Pastor told me the oil washes off but the cross doesn't.

I ran to the mirror when I got home. I wanted to see my cross. It was really faint but I thought I could see it.

We had a party for our baptism. Grandma gave me my own Bible. She told me to read it to Joel. He was too little to know how to handle books.

Mom put our baptism candles on the shelf. She said we would light them every year on January 10, the day we were baptized.

That night, after the party, Dad helped me wash up for bed. He washed away the oil. He said, "Don't worry, your cross will never go away. You are baptized. You are God's child forever."

The next day, I checked my forehead and Joel's. I couldn't see our crosses, but I knew they were there. I traced my finger over the cross on Joel's head. I told him, "Don't worry, your cross will never go away!"

When Joel turned one year old, we had a party for him. He sat in his high chair and Mom put the cake in front of him. It had one candle. Everybody said, "Blow out the candle, Joel!" He couldn't do it, so I helped. I even made the wish for him. I had to help him open his presents, too. I think Joel liked his party, even though he was just a baby.

This year, he was two. He blew out the candles all by himself. He ripped off the paper to open his presents. I still made the wish for him, though, just in case he couldn't do that yet.

Soon after Joel's birthday is Thanksgiving.
This year, I ate Thanksgiving dinner at the big
table with the grown-ups. Grandma had me sit
on a phone book. She put out a fancy tablecloth
made of lace. I could tell it was very special to
her. I decided I would try extra hard not to spill
on it.

Everything at the table was special. My older
cousins put out flowers and tiny pumpkins and
candles. It looked beautiful.

In the kitchen, I helped stir the mashed pota-
toes. I put some jelly into a bowl to help
Grandma. She said it was special jelly to eat
with our turkey, not the kind of jelly you put on
bread!

At dinner, I tried the jelly. It tasted funny all
by itself. I spread the rest on my roll and ate it
when she wasn't looking.

Uncle Jess said the blessing for our Thanksgiving dinner. He took a lon-n-n-g time. He said he was thankful for our family. He was thankful for our country. He was thankful for all the good food.

My cousin Benjamin whispered, "Why doesn't he just say 'Come, Lord Jesus, be our guest' like we always do at home?" I told him that you had to have special prayers for special meals.

When Uncle Jess was finally done praying, we both said, "Amen."

Joel sat in the high chair while Dad cut turkey into little pieces for him. Joel threw some of his food on the floor. That made Benjamin laugh, but I knew that some of the grown-ups didn't think it was very funny. Joel still has to learn how to behave at the table, especially at special meals.

"Did you bring me to Thanksgiving dinner when I was two?" I asked Dad.

"Of course!" he said. "This is a family meal. You are part of our family. And Joel is part of our family."

That night, when it was time for bedtime
prayers, Mom said we should say "thank-you"
prayers. I said, "Thank you, God, for my family.
Thank you for letting Joel come to Thanksgiving, even if he doesn't know how to behave.
And thanks for the jelly, I guess." Before she left
the room, Mom traced a cross on my forehead
with her finger. "Remember, God loves you,"
she said.

JESUS IS HERE

My Bible is full of stories about God and Jesus. Many of them are surprising and exciting! My favorite stories tell how God and Jesus loved people—caring for them, forgiving them, blessing them.

I try to read my Bible to Joel. When I first got it, I couldn't read very well. Now, I can read better, but some of the words are still hard.

My Bible has pictures in it, so I show Joel the pictures. Sometimes, Joel just wants to turn the pages really fast.

Joel knows Jesus, though. I showed him all the pictures of Jesus. Now he points to the picture and says, "Jesus! Jesus!"

One of the stories I read to Joel is about the Lord's Supper. The night before Jesus died on the cross, Jesus and his disciples gathered to eat the Passover meal. While they were eating, Jesus told them of a wonderful surprise.

During the meal Jesus took some bread in his hands. He blessed the bread and broke it. Then he gave it to his disciples and said, "Take this and eat it. This is my body."

Jesus picked up a cup of wine and gave thanks to God. He then gave it to his disciples and said, "Take this and drink it. This is my blood, . . . poured out, so that many people will have their sins forgiven" (Matthew 26:26-28 CEV).

Ever since that night long ago, Jesus' followers have gathered to eat the bread and drink the wine of the Lord's Supper. Jesus told the disciples that the bread and the wine are his body and his blood. Sometimes it's hard to understand how bread and wine can also be Jesus' body and blood. But the Bible promises that this is true. It is one of God's loving surprises!

14

I told Joel about what happened on Easter, after Jesus had died on the cross. The women went to the place where Jesus was buried. It was Sunday morning. The rock was rolled away and Jesus' body was gone.

Suddenly two men in shining clothes stood beside them. The women were afraid and bowed to the ground. But the men said, "Why are you looking in the place of the dead for someone who is alive? Jesus is not here! He has been raised from death" (Luke 24:4b-6a CEV).

"That's why we go to church on Sunday, Joel," I said. "Jesus came alive on a Sunday. Now, Jesus is with us every time we have Communion." I know Joel doesn't understand everything I tell him. He likes the pictures, though.

When we go to church, Joel sometimes gets fussy and makes noise. Mom says I used to be like that, too. I've been trying to teach Joel how to act in church. It's hard.

Sometimes worship seems so long, but I like the feeling of being in God's house. I look at the baptismal font. I remember that I am God's child forever. I think about that invisible cross I have on my forehead.

Now I take Holy Communion. At our church, we call our altar the Welcome Table. We sing a song about the Welcome Table. We eat the food Jesus has given us.

When I come to the Welcome Table, I remember how Jesus gave bread and wine to his disciples. I think about the surprising promises God makes to us in this meal! At the Lord's Supper, God tells us that our sins are forgiven. Because Jesus died on the cross, God will not punish us for the things we should not do. And Jesus promises that his body and blood will give us life with him in heaven after we die.

THE WELCOME TABLE

Last Sunday, I invited my friend Amanda to come to church with me. She didn't know anything about church. I had to teach her everything!

"When the worship begins, we stand up to show respect for God," I told Amanda. I shared the book with her.

"When we pray, it's like talking to God," I told her. "Close your eyes and bow your head. It's easier to hear the prayers that way."

During the offering, I whispered to Amanda about Communion. "You won't eat yet because you aren't baptized. But you can come to the Welcome Table with me anyway. Pastor will give you a blessing. It's really special because Jesus comes to us in the bread and the wine.

Amanda looked around and said, "I don't see Jesus."

"I know, but he's there just the same," I explained. "When you get baptized, you'll get a cross on your forehead, just like mine."

Amanda looked at me and scratched her head. "I don't see any cross," she whispered.

"I know, but it's there. You'll find out," I said.

The helper started setting the table. "It's a special meal, kind of like Thanksgiving," I whispered. "See the white tablecloth? See the special dishes?"

The helper put a tall cup on the cloth and lifted a napkin to uncover some small loaves of bread. He poured some wine into the cup.

"That's not very much food for all these people!" said Amanda.

I giggled just a little and said, "We just get a taste of the food. When we are in heaven, there will be a big Welcome Table with a whole feast. Everybody will eat together with Jesus. Even people who have died. Even enemies." Amanda's eyes got really big.

Pastor said the long blessing prayer she always says before Holy Communion is served. Usually, I think it is boring, like my Uncle Jess's Thanksgiving prayers. But I really listened this time. I was trying to help Amanda understand.

The prayer told all about the great things God has done. It told about how Jesus gave himself for us on the cross. I told Amanda, "Listen." She kept looking at the bread and the cup and Pastor.

When it was our turn to come to the Welcome Table, Amanda watched me while I ate the bread and drank the wine. She winked. I think she wondered if Jesus was really there.

Then Pastor gave Amanda a blessing. Amanda had a big smile on her face. Some other kids from our school were also around the Table. They recognized Amanda and gave little waves. I held Amanda's hand as we walked back to our seats.

While the people were singing, I said, "I hope you can come to the Welcome Table all the time. I think Jesus would like you to."

"Will they teach me more about Jesus at Sunday school?" asked Amanda.

"Sure," I said, "That's where we go next. Now, shhh! Here comes my favorite part!"

The whole church got very quiet. I looked up at my little brother, in Dad's arms. "I've been teaching Joel this," I whispered to Amanda. "Listen."

The helper held out his hands and said, "Go in peace. Serve the Lord." Joel and I looked at each other and said in our biggest voices, "Thanks be to God!"

DEAR PARENTS . . .

Here are some ways to continue the conversation with your child after reading each part of this book.

Special Days, Special Meals

Look for mementos of your child's baptismal day such as photos, cards, certificate, and candle. Children are often very interested in seeing the baptismal clothing they wore, too. Plan a special observance of his or her next baptismal anniversary.

Teach your child to trace his or her baptismal cross to remember that he or she is God's child forever. Martin Luther encouraged people to do this upon waking in the morning, before grace at meals, at bedtime, and at the beginning of worship.

Talk about special meals in your family, such as birthdays and Thanksgiving. Remind your child of the ways he or she is included in your family activities.

Talk about manners for different settings, such as mealtime and worship. Help your child notice how he or she has grown in ability to behave in these situations. Think of ways to encourage your child to participate in appropriate new ways.

Jesus Is Here

Get out a Bible and read the scripture selections referred to in this book. Read also the second chapter of Luke, about the birth and childhood of Jesus.

Talk together about the amazing power of God's love and forgiveness in these stories. Emphasize the importance of Jesus' promise that his body and blood (present in, with, and under the bread and wine of Holy Communion) will bring forgiveness and life everlasting. This is one of God's wonderful and loving surprises!

Encourage your child to read or show pictures from the Bible to a younger sibling or friend. Consult your pastor or parish educator for advice in choosing a suitable children's picture Bible.

Establish a simple bedtime routine of Bible reading and prayer. A devotional booklet for children and families, such as *The Home Altar* (Augsburg Fortress) can be helpful.

The Welcome Table

Together, sing "The Welcome Table," at the back of this book. Talk together about those with whom you would like to feast at the heavenly Welcome Table.

Talk about your child's participation in Holy Communion. Find out what your child delights in and hopes for during worship. Do you have specific plans for when he or she will begin to receive Holy Communion? Help your child look ahead with joy.

Provide an opportunity for your child to invite an unchurched friend to worship. Encourage your child to teach the guest about Jesus and about how to act in church.